The Bigfoot Parchments

Richard Rensberry

Copyright © 2021, Richard Rensberry

All rights reserved.

No part of this publication may be reproduced, stored in a retrieval system or transmitted in any form or by any means electronic, mechanical, photo-copied, recorded or otherwise, without the prior written permission of the publisher and authors.

Published by: QuickTurtle Books LLC®

https://www.conversationswithsasquatch.com

ISBN: 978-1-940736-69-3

Published in the United States of America

This book is dedicated to the land of Cross Over* and the shared knowledge of the Sasquatch.

Cross Over- Parallel land of the Sasquatch

Contents

Title Page 3
Copyright Page 4
Dedication Page 5
Contents 7-8
Preface 9
Acknowledgements 11
Title Page 13
Note To Reader 14
The Bigfoot Parchments 15
Bigfoot Parchment #1 17-18
Blurry Photo 19
The Afterglow 21
Bigfoot Parchment #2 23-24
High Diver 25
Cross Over 27
Bigfoot Parchment #3 29-30
As We See It 31
Bigfoot's Choice 33
Bigfoot Parchment #4 35
The Labyrinth 37
From the Heart of the Forest 39
Bigfoot Parchment #5 41
Celebration 43
The Feast 45
Bigfoot Parchment #6 47-48
Kenaf 49
Festival 51
Bigfoot Parchment #7 53
The Portal 55
Bigfoot 57
Bigfoot Parchment #8 59
Chiha Tanka Dance 61
Wolves 63
Bigfoot Parchment #9 65
Rebels 67
The Exiled 69

Bigfoot Parchment #10   71
The Joke   73
Legend   75
Bigfoot Parchment #11   77
Bigfoot Names   79
Bigfoot Vows   81
Bigfoot Parchment #12   83
The Awakening   85
The Forest   87
Bigfoot Parchment #13   89
Tea   91
Bee Keeper   93
Bigfoot Parchment #14   95
Friends   97
The Sculptor   99
Bigfoot Parchment #15   101
Forest Meadow   103
The Gift   105
Bigfoot Parchment #16   107
The Few   109
The Encounter   111
Bigfoot Parchment #17   113
The Crepuscule   115
Spear Fisherman   117
Bigfoot Parchment #18   119
Secrets   121
Lake Pariseema   123
Bigfoot Parchment #19   125
Bigfoot Parchment #20   127
Bigfoot Parchment #21   129
Glossary   130-133
Other Sasquatch Books   134
Review Request   135
Conversations With Sasquatch, The Encounter   137-139

PREFACE

The ***Bigfoot Parchments*** were given to me during my journey and prolonged stay in Cross Over, the land of the Sasquatch. Rutheeus, Member of the Sasquatch Council of Elders, entrusted me with the Bigfoot knowledge contained in these parchments as a means for helping mankind. The nature of these parchments and their significance to helping mankind is the subject of Book 3, ***The Awakening***, in my ***Conversations With Sasquatch*** series of novels. This ***Bigfoot Parchments*** book delivers the Parchments in the raw.

Acknowledgments

I would like to thank Kenaf Partners USA for their valuable knowledge and research into the kenaf plant. I would also like to thank Dr. Richard Olree for his contribution to the knowledge and research of the minerals necessary for blocking the spread of Covid 19.

I'd also like to thank my readers that have followed my online Bigfoot novels. Your comments have been a guiding light. A special thanks to my lovely wife, Mary, for her undoubting courage and support.

The Bigfoot Parchments

Richard Rensberry

Note To Reader

There is a glossary of Sasquatch terms and unusual words at the back of this book.

If you do not understand a word, it will block your understanding of the concept in which the word is used. The definitions of words are here for your reference and benefit. Thank you.

Richard Rensberry, Author

The Bigfoot Parchments

There are no hieroglyphs
nor painted rocks in caves;
no fossils of Bigfoot remains.

The Bigfoot exist
in the dimension of trees
and speak the language of rivers
and meandering streams.

They are seers and poets…
sculptors with gifts
from a world of dreams. They are philosophers
of source. They have
deciphered the secrets
of where thoughts were born.

I have the parchments to prove it…
the inherent wisdom of their ancient souls,
their knowledge of seeds,
roots, and livingness. They hold the keys
to the holy grail.

Bigfoot Parchment #1

The secret of time

This text is accompanied by an illustration as follows:

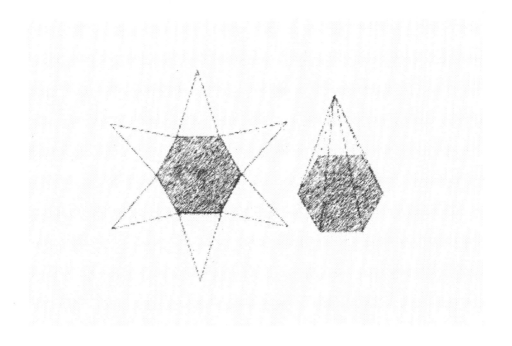

"It is the law of how two worlds can occupy the same space. In other words, space is not made of time. Space is not bound, it is limitless, so it exists outside the realm of time. That is what you humans have forgotten. You are a race lost in time." Rutheeus, Member of the Sasquatch Council of Elders.

"If you take the star points and fold them all vertically, you have a perfect teepee. A teepee is sister to The Stone Without Time*. It's a spirit catcher. It preserves our memories and passes them down. I have claimed the memories of my father and my mother from my family's teepee, and the memories of their fathers and mothers before them. Time does not exist in the realm of the spirit." Tecumseh, my Native American friend.

The Stone Without Time- Lapis Lazuli stone gifted to me by the Sasquatch Loquius that holds visions of the past present and future.

Blurry Photo

Through a veil of morning fog
Bigfoot appears like a mirage.

Huge muscles ripple
beneath a shimmering coat
of blue-black hues.

Phantom man
with cunning eyes like gemstones.

For an instant he stands
perfectly still…. framed in my lens.

The Afterglow

With the orb of the moon
haloed and blushing,
two Sasquatch stroll
with fingers laced. Enticed
by the meadow's magic
of fireflies sparking,
they pause to embrace.

Hungry kisses
beneath the bows of larch.
A negligee of wispy fog
on a bed of pippsissewa.*
A chorus of moans…
and an owl's screech…
eerie cries of howling wolves…

crescendo and peace.

*pippsissewa- Native American name for the wintergreen plant.

Bigfoot Parchment #2

The is of what is is is

This basic truth is accompanied by a painting of our beautiful planet Earth floating in a galactic sea.

"If something is true it is true. It doesn't matter what someone's opinion might be, it cannot change the reality of truth. It can change a law or another's opinion, but it cannot change the is of what is." Rutheeus, Member of the Sasquatch Council of Elders

"The is of what is is observable. It is not thoughts about the observable nor ideas about something observable, it is the actual observation. You could look at a tree and see the limbs of the tree are moving. The only observable fact is the limbs of the tree are moving. If you then said it is windy based on the observation that the limbs of the tree are moving, that is not necessarily the truth of what is. It could actually be calm and the limbs are moving because there's a Bigfoot grasping the tree and shaking it. Or maybe there's some kind of bird or animal that is making the tree limbs move instead of the wind. Truth cannot be acquired by conjecture or guess work, it has to be observed as it is, or it is just opinion and thinkingness. That is the problem with justice systems, they are rarely administered on truth." Loquius, Master at Arms for the Sasquatch Council of Elders

High Diver

The Rogue River gorge
erupts with thunder
where rapids squeezed
form big blue walls
of misted granite. Along the rim
of descending pools
are Bigfoot prints
and a pile of scat
repugnant with fish. Further on,
where the water falls
some thirty feet, a Sasquatch stands
with lifted arms and knees bent.... a spring coiled,
poised to leap.

Cross Over

It's a place I go
to get out of the wind
of bad news and imbeciles;
it's a far place
beyond skepticism…
its ambiance is Bigfeet
on imperial moss, its voice
is raw timber
and the sooth of Sasquatch. Its roof
is lit by billions
of stars that make you teeter
totter and faint.

It's a place I go
but it's home to Bigfeet.

Bigfoot Parchment #3

Nothing is by coincidence

The parchment picture associated with this concept is an empty circle, or a zero.

$$0$$

"In the language of math, it is the equivalent of the denominator that cancels out every numerator by being equal. In other words, taking responsibility for your own actions or inactions leaves absolutely nothing to which justifications or lies can attach themselves. **Nothing is by coincidence.**" Deutonius member of the Sasquatch Council of Elders

"Things don't come to be by coincidence. They come to be because of being created by the internal and external forces present at that moment." Loquius, Master at Arms for the Sasquatch Council of Elders

This concept first threw me for a loop. But I have come to see that this follows the Sasquatch law of: *The is of what is is is.*

Things don't come to be by coincidence. They come to be because they are created by someone's actions or inactions.

An example of this is: If two cars collide it is not by coincidence. It is not a coincidence or an accident that someone is texting and drifts across the centerline and hits another car. That collision was caused. To believe otherwise is in direct violation of Parchment #2.

This is an intriguing truth so easily dismissed by us blame-minded humans, because accepting responsibility for such an all consuming statement is hard to fathom.

As We See It

"Our reality is bound
only by thought. Our world is big
or our world is naught. It is
as we conceive it."

      Loquius, My Sasquatch Friend

Bigfoot's Choice

Before the computer
made Bill Gates God,
and Zuckerberg
the fairy fact checker....

there were sooth
talkers and magicians.

Bigfoot Parchment # 4

The answer to complexity is simple

The illustration for this concept on the parchment is a straight line.

_____

"If things are complex, then there has been thinkingness introduced to confound that observable reality. Life in its natural state of truth is simple. It is composed of what's there, not what you think is there." Rutheeus, Member of the Sasquatch Council of Elders

I love these Sasquatch Parchments for this reason. They are basic truths that bear more fruit than my 20 years of human institutional schooling. *The answer to complexity is simple.*

The Labyrinth

It is a proverb
that the Sasquatch are innately wise.
They know how truth
is the torch that leads
out of the labyrinth composed of lies.

Even humans sometimes listen
to their conscience speak
behind the cacophony
of voices within their lives. Call them
angels or call them warriors
with axes, guns and knives.

From The Heart of the Forest

There is an entity among trees,
an omniscient keeper
of the air above
and the earth beneath. Sasquatch,
whose being speaks, listens and sees
beyond the intrusion of man's disdain,
a guardian of the forest
with a kiss and a fist
like God.

Bigfoot Parchment # 5

Eyes have vision
The soul behind those eyes
is knowingness and sight
before they see

The illustration for this parchment is a circle with a line through it. It looks very much like the greek symbol Theta.

"Precognition or knowingness exists without the use of one's physical eyes." Loquius, Master at Arms for the Sasquatch Council of Elders.

Celebration

On Christmas Day
put an ear to a maple
or birch and listen…. you'll hear
the bells of Cross Over ring
through the trees of the forest
where the Bigfoot reign.

They are the bells from a hammer
to chisel to stone, the bells of a clapper
carved out of bone.
They are the bells of Leeitus*
and the bells of Pariseema*, the toll
of Awakening in a brand new world.

They are the bells of the Elders
from the Temple of Cheer…. the bells of a harkening
and the bells to concur
the best is yet to come.

*Leeitus- son of Loquius, Master at Arms for the Sasquatch Council of Elders

*Pariseema- Lake on which the Sasquatch city of Pariseema is built

The Feast

When harvests are bountiful
and the horizon glows,
the Sasquatch gather
with fiddles and bows.

They chant and clap
each rhythm and rhyme,
gossip and sip
spiked juice of the lime.

They sing old songs
of passed down sooth…
nurture the hopes
of love struck youth.

They pat sore backs
of friends and foes,
snap their fingers
and tap big toes.

There's plenty for all
when they stomp their feet;
hoot and holler
to come and eat.

Bigfoot Parchment # 6

Seeds and roots are the beginning of change

This parchment is illustrated with a germinating seed.

"Seeds and roots are filled with the energy of life. They're miracles of abundance, perceived and realized each and every day of our lives. Like ourselves, seeds and roots are immortal, a model of life nurturing life." Deutonius, member of the Sasquatch Council of Elders

"Our thoughts and intentions are no different than the miracles of seeds and roots. Their inception has the power to change anything and everything for the better. That is the purpose of thought. It is not to remain static or change things for the worse. Those kinds of thoughts are the seeds for disaster, for famine and war, the seeds and roots of destruction." Rutheeus, Member of the Sasquatch Council of Elders

As humans, these simple words should be enough to change our minds; to plant the seeds and roots of worthwhile goals and purposes.

Kenaf

Kenaf is sown
for fibers to weave
into parchment and linens,
into filaments for fishing,
into fisherman's baskets
and picnic mats,
into kayaks and nets….

everything needed
for a Bigfoot quest .

Festival

Seeds hold miracles
of life in a shell. A sunflower,
a daisy, a radish or corn
just waiting for warmth
and a place to be born.

In the womb of the forest
where Sasquatch conceive…
sprout wondrous kenaf
and gooseberry trees, artichoke hearts
and asparagus stalks, plums
and roots of licorice…. everything
from the Earth's boutique.

Bigfoot Parchment # 7

*Truth cannot be added to
nor subtracted from
to make it what it is*

This parchment's illustration is that of a tree.

"A tree is a tree no matter what. You can cut off a limb and it still is a tree. If you destroy it there is always its seed." Loquius, Master at Arms for the Sasquatch Council of Elders

I can see that we humans try very hard to add and subtract from the truth, especially when we are guilty.

The Portal

There's an anomaly
where the compass fails
in the old woods
near Big Creek. North ain't north
and south ain't south. East and west
get flipped on their heads.

I, who never gets lost
got lost here…. where the water runs
backwards, then repeats itself
over and over
like a line in a song.

It's where the hairs
on your neck get tickled….
where your mouth grows dry
and you hold your breath.

It is the longitude
and latitude of Bigfoot —
my Sasquatch friend.

Bigfoot

Their teeth are square
to pulverize roots, nuts and vegetables.
They are farmers of fruits
and heirloom crops. The Sasquatch
avoid all flesh except fresh fish. Their hair is coarse
like a horse's mane, it keeps them warm
and sheds the rain. They live at peace
in a forest where they beat their drums
with Bigfoot hands. They sing and chant.
Their eyes like gems are deep-set
in a large head — cunning and intelligent
benevolent masters of wit and stealth.
The invisible man.

Bigfoot Parchment # 8

Facts are whittled by opinions into lies

This parchment has the illustration of a stone bird

This illustration reminds me of our human main stream media in exactitude. They no longer report facts but opinions that result in stone birds that don't fly.

Chiha Tanka Dance

To the Ojibwa
and the Chippewa he was magical
and wily as the fox. Sasquatch…
brother to the Spirit of the Wolf.
A being full of power
to be summoned by the drum to dance
for man's Awakening
out of war, famine and drought.

Wolves

You can't fool a wolf
even with scents
like pine tar or sage
on boot bottoms.
They smell your intent
and perk their ears
at the beat of your heart.

They are the forest's skin
covered with fur. They are
the howl of the wounded
and the carnivore's teeth…
but bow to the pet
and coo of Bigfoot.

Bigfoot Parchment # 9

Our greatest weapon is the power of intent

This concept is illustrated by an empty thought bubble.

I guess is it is ours into which to put our best of intentions.

Rebels

Teen angst
has no bounds, color or creed,
even among Sasquatch exiled
into a world of men.

The Exiled

Even the Bigfoot have apples go sour,
eaters of mushrooms
like amanita muscaria, drinkers
of moonshine and poppers of pills.

These big boy rebels
are renegade thugs,
the window peepers and shadow creatures
from a nightmare on drugs.

Even the Sasquatch use judges,
juries and jail.
The worst get exiled
to where humans prevail… but

most Sasquatch are gentle benevolent souls
that wish us well and leave us alone.

Bigfoot Parchment # 10

Action is the source of energy

This parchment is represented by the flowing of a river.

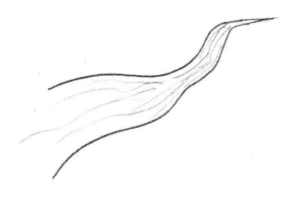

"It is a common misconception that action takes energy. It is the direct opposite that is true." Amish wiseman

The Joke

Have you ever heard
a Sasquatch laugh?
Well, I'd call it a cackle
at unbelievability, a derisive
interjection
composed of sarcasm
and a shake of the head.

They think we're a joke.

Legend

There's a legend that speaks
of a stone called Reason. A stone
without time in which Sasquatch resides
and speaks to us from
an outpost in eternity.

It is the stone of perceptions
and the quest of our visions.
It is the stone of our Earth
and her breath everlasting.
It is the stone of our burdens

that can't be denied.

Bigfoot Parchment # 11

There is no darkness at the source of light

This knowledge is illustrated with a brilliant sunburst.

Bigfoot Names

In the Temple of Cheer
each birth has its stone,
a permanent mark
and symbolic role

for strength, wisdom
and capability.

The stone is named
and placed in prayer
to bear the weight
of all eternity.

Bigfoot Vows

Today there's a wedding
in the Temple of Cheer.
Young Leeitus will join
his hand with hers.
Their vows are eternal
for kiss and caress,
their love is monogamous....
promises professed.

Bigfoot Parchment # 12

We are an expression of possibility

The illustration for this parchment is a star.

I believe it means anything is possible. That would mean nothing is impossible.

The Awakening

The journey
from the beginning
was to begin

our sacred role as caretakers
of life in the forests, of rivers that cleanse
and the seeds that feed us.

It is our duty to imbue
life not death…. to grant sentience
to stone and bird alike. Yes, it is Sasquatch duty
to respect and give space
even to the weasel and snake. But most of all

it is our burden to wake
the human race.

The Forest

The tranquil hush
of heavy wet snow, no breeze
in a rush to intrude, just beauty
conceived and perceived
in the house of the Sasquatch.

Bigfoot Parchment # 13

Ability is command over all space and all objects

This parchment is illustrated with a Sasquatch house.

Tea

From the mighty forest's

stores of raspberry,
jasmine and dandelion,
Loquiili makes tea.

From the fruits
of pear, sweet apple
and pin cherry,

from the stores of juniper,
rose and burdock,

from the mighty forest's

kenaf and licorice,
peppermint and chamomile,

sap of maple,
birch and bitters,
Loquiili makes tea.

The Sasquatch sip
and dunk their biscuits.

Bee Keeper

From flowers to bees
laden with pollen,
the woodlands are blessed
with hollow tree nests
and underground combs
of lip licking best
honey. Honey

is currency
in the Bigfoot bank.
Honey buys passion
and honey buys thanks.

Honey gives Bigfoot
bee keepers rank.

From the wildest blossoms
of pink and red rose,
to the bumble of bees
and the caw of the crows,
the forest is Bigfoot
bee keeper's gold.

Bigfoot Parchment # 14

Invisibility is the ability to create and destroy space

The illustration is a dotted line.

— —

Now you see them, now you don't. It is a game the Sasquatch play with other life forms and us less spiritually endowed humans.

Friends

At the source of all
is purity, clever little miracles
in the puzzle of creation.

The river is one.
It lives for the future
and never looks back
at what it's done.

Another is winter.
It bears perseverance
and always looks ahead
to the beauty of spring.

Yet another is the sky
deciding to be infinite
as the wind. God's music
to my Sasquatch friends.

The Sculptor

With hands forming lives
unto themselves
he shapes blue clay
into a face. The face of a fox
or a mad wolverine, the face
of an owl or a face of a hawk.

With hammer and blade
he chisels and draws
the features of wolves
or a fellow Sasquatch.
Chips a rock into flocks
of sparrows and crows.
Totems a tree
into the likeness of foes
such as cougar and bear.

With lever and stone
he molds a sphere…
to praise and give birth
to a prosperous Earth.

Bigfoot Parchment # 15

Intention is father to creation

This parchment is illustrated by closed eyes.

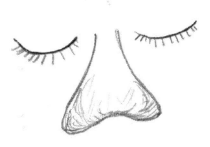

"All life vibrates according to its intention. Those vibrations are a language of their own. Life is but an attempt to decipher and define those vibrations and frequencies emitted by the being himself and not the illusions of its physical form." Deutonius, Member of the Sasquatch Council of Elders.

Forest Meadow

The artist of spring
is out painting poppies,
blue bells and ferns

where little Bigfeet frolic
with a fox in a game
of sneak-a-boo peek. Look out
for Momma
where ever she is.

The Gift

A stone shaped like a heart
was left on my doorstep.
It came in the night
without fanfare or fuss.
It came as a gift
on little feet, by way of the forest
and a child named Pureesis. A princess
of a smitten Sasquatch.

Bigfoot Parchment # 16

Combined good intentions can destroy any problem

The illustration for this concept is:

$$1 + 1 + 1 = 0$$

"Since problems are created by counter intentions of self or others, directing intentions towards constructive results creates an abundance of directed intentions or solutions. The problem will vanish." Loquius, Master at Arms for the Sasquatch Council of Elders.

This is the finger that points at me.

The Few

We see them
in our mind's eye,
these abominable giants of the forest,
perpetrators of legends, folktales
and scary beliefs…. hairy beasts
that would tear us apart
with powerful jaws and teeth.

I have never encountered such a savage cliche,
only a Bigfoot daddy, momma
and family. I have been in their home
and shared fruits, vegetables and tea. Philosophically
they are highly intelligent
and way superior to me.

I liken it to a life among the Amish,
where beings abhor cameras,
electromagnetic waves and technology.
The Sasquatch enjoy fishing, farming
and church…. excepting a few
rebels angered by the ignorance
and arrogance of man.

The Encounter

We share
the same stars,
moon and sun,
even the same Earth
shifted in time and space
by a different pair of feet.
Sometimes however, somehow
we meet.

Bigfoot Parchment # 17

Mind reading is listening to the language of intent

This parchment has an illustration of an ear with a slash through it.

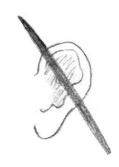

"Common sense and gut feeling is not listening to words but to the intent behind those words. It is seeing without eyes and hearing without ears. It is perceptions beyond the physical body honed by knowing instead of looking." Rutheeus, Member of the Sasquatch Council of Elders

"Life is often a battle between the opposing intentions of greater good and greater evil. The ability to read intentions and vibrations is an ability of utmost importance in life. Thus reading minds is not a sixth sense, it is the first sense for a successfully intended life." Loquius, Master at Arms for the Sasquatch Council of Elders

The Crepuscule

At the hour of dusk
the forest falls silent
and reminiscent of the day's success
with birds trilling in the thickets
and the crickets screeching
bows and fiddles near Big Creek.

It is the hour of prayer
and serene contemplation.
For the Sasquatch, an affirmation
for being blessed, a rebirth
of Earth's perfections, of visions
to create a tomorrow filled with love
and abundance for all.

Spear Fisherman

Spring fed McKinley
holds rainbows and browns
in a bosom of silence
broken only by loons.

Big trout slurp
the surface near shore
where Bigfoot stands
dead still as a stork....

Bigfoot Parchment # 18

Worlds exist as manifestations of intent

This concept is once again illustrated by the Earth floating in a galactic sea.

"What one does and has in life is the result of intentions. The intentions of himself foremost and the influence of others as well. If one intends happiness he will attract happiness and go about creating it. If one intends chaos he will attract and create chaos. If one intends to build a house the house will be built. If he intends not to build a house there will be no house." Rutheeus, Member of the Sasquatch Council of Elders

Secrets

If you believe Sasquatch
to be an animal,
he most likely will accost you.
If your mind is made up
that he smells like a skunk, he'll blatantly
stink you. If you treat him
like a dumb ass, he'll deceive
and elude your presence
for eternity. If you treat him as an equal
he will tell you secrets
of the universe.

Lake Pariseema

At the hour of dawn
the moon hangs blue.
The boats are out
and on the move.
The Sasquatch cast
seine nets and lines
with intent to catch
a sturgeon prize.

The Elders bow
to praise the sun
and say goodbye
to stars above.
The children race
in games of tag
then mount their wolves
to storm the day.

I tie my shoes
and steal away.

Bigfoot Parchment # 19

When outside equals inside there can exist a thing called freedom

This concept is illustrated by an equal sign.

$$=$$

"You can't deceive yourself and expect to be free of deception." Ted Kaczynski, the Unabomber

Bigfoot Parchment #20

In order for betrayal to exist one has to first betray

This concept is illustrated with two opposing arrows

"I have thought long and hard on this concept. I think betrayal is probably the most dangerous and damaging of vibrations. It can corrupt the best of intentions. It can change the vibration of good into evil. It is the vibration of politics and the manifestation of conflict. Betrayal of self or one's own integrity of knowingness is the cause of man's current state of mind-reading blindness. He has lost his most important sense and has come to believe it doesn't even exist.

To the Sasquatch it is as real as we are now blind."
Richard Rensberry, Author.

Bigfoot Parchment #21

Life is not divisible into itself

The picture that's associated with this concept is once again a painting of planet Earth floating in a galactic sea. The exact same painting that has described more than one concept from the parchments.

I am sure it probably has more significance than I can fathom, but the gist of that significance means to me that life is a whole. It means planet Earth is a living being unto itself. It is not divisible if it is to remain healthy and whole. You cannot destroy any of its parts unless you want problems with all the other parts. You pollute the air and you pollute everything. You poison the bugs and you poison yourself.

Glossary of Terms

abhor- dislike greatly

ad infinitum- endlessly, forever

ambiance- quality of setting or surroundings, nature

anomaly- departure from normal

arbitrary- based on one's preference, bias or whim

benevolent- kindliness, intention to do good

blatantly- in a conspicuous and obtrusive way

boutique- a store with unique items

Chiha Tanka- Bigfoot or Sasquatch

Chippewa- Native American tribe present in Michigan

cliche- overused or trite idea

crepuscule- dusk

Cross Over- the world of the Sasquatch that butts up against ours to create portals

derisive- in a manner of contempt, ridicule

harkening- a calling to come or gather

heirloom- seeds handed down from generation to generation

hieroglyphs- picture writing

holy grail- cup used by Jesus at the Last Supper and by Joseph to collect drops of blood from Jesus at his Crucifixion, the cup of knowledge

imbeciles- very foolish or stupid people

inherent- inborn, existing in someone or something as a natural state

kenaf- a hibiscus plant used for many worthwhile purposes by the Sasquatch and being successfully used by humans for those same worthwhile purposes

labyrinth- complicated and perplexing state of affairs

larch- a conifer tree that sheds its needles in winter

Leeitus- son of the Sasquatch Loquius

Loquiili- wife of Sasquatch Loquius

mirage- a figment or phantom reality, hallucination

naught- nothing

Ojibwa- Native American tribe present in Michigan

omniscient- knowing all things, infinite knowledge

orb- a spherical object

parchments- the skin of an animal prepared as a surface for writing or painting. A sheet of parchment used in this way, documents or manuscripts

Pariseema- Sasquatch home to the council of Elders and center of trade

pippsissewa- Native American name for the wintergreen plant

poised- in a position to, ready

proverb- obvious truth

repugnant- disagreeable or revolting

Rutheeus- Sasquatch Elder, Master at Arms for the Council of Elders located in Pariseema, Cross Over

scat- poop

seers- visionaries, those that see without eyes

skepticism- doubting in attitude or state of mind, not believing

sooth- truth

static- unmoving or unchanged

Stone Without Time- magical stone gifted to me by Loquius.

Temple of Cheer- Temple in Pariseema, Cross Over

whittled- cut away

Other Books in The Conversations With Sasquatch Series

Conversations with Sasquatch,
The Encounter

Conversations With Sasquatch,
Cross Over

available on Amazon or at:
store.booksmakebooms.com

If you enjoyed this book please visit it on Amazon and leave a review to help others with your precious words. It means a lot to Indie authors like myself.

The following is the opening chapter of
Conversations With Sasquatch, The Encounter
My first Sasquatch Novel

1

I have had to readjust my beliefs and rethink many an opinion since I met a Sasquatch while out hunting for morel mushrooms in Lewiston, Michigan. I had no idea that these mushrooms were high on their list of dietary delicacies. They prize and love them.

I would have been afraid and crapped my pants if it hadn't been for the long outstretched arm that offered me a half eaten morel. There was nothing aggressive or hostile in this gesture. He effused a welcoming aura of curious friendliness.

I took the half-eaten morel and popped it into my mouth. As I shook my head affirmatively, I offered him my paper sack that contained about twenty morels and two or three beefsteaks I had gathered along a cedar ridge beside Big Creek.

It was then that I noticed the pure silence that had fallen over the forest. The crows look-out caws had vanished, the squirrels had shushed their chatter and rattle in the trees. Not even a bluejay or a mosquito was daring a peep.

I struggled to swallow the copper taste that had encroached to dry my mouth.

Sasquatch smiled. He had jaws filled with yellow teeth and eyes that twinkled with delight.

"Thank you," he said, and jiggled his lips like a horse as it eats a sugar cube off your hand.

"You're welcome," I replied with another swallow.

"There's a storm in the air," Sasquatch offered with a gesture towards the sky, "the ozone is lifting my hairs." He proceeded to run his hand a few inches above his upper chest where I could see the hairs stand up as if a magnet were being run over a cache of metal shavings. He abruptly slapped his chest and laughed. It sounded eerily like the shriek of an eagle guarding its kill.

The sky was clear, but I thought I could hear a distant rumble of thunder to the west. I couldn't remember any rain being in the forecast. I had come dressed only in jeans, a polo shirt and sneakers.

"You humans are such frail creatures," he said. "I remember when you were more like us, hunters and gatherers of the health and fruits of The Creator."

I really couldn't tell if he was speaking to me verbally or telepathically. There was such a sense of otherworldliness. I had a hard time getting a grip on my racing thoughts and emotions. In the absence of abject fear, I felt a combination of elation and serenity. I guess it was what you'd call dumbstruck.

"Not much of a talker, are you?" he asked and popped a fresh mushroom into his mouth.

"I have never met a Sasquatch before," I managed.

"Not many a human has," he whispered conspiratorially. "You are the first in many thousands of years I have spoken to. You are the chosen one."

"I am honored," I humbly croaked.

"I am not so sure you should be. You humans are blowing it. You are blind to the world of the Sasquatch. You have lost the memory and instinct of your body's genes and the very essence of your immortal soul."

A darkness crept stealthily over the ridge. Lightning flashed and a huge clap of thunder reverberated off and rattled my teeth. I began to shiver uncontrollably as Sasquatch melted into the rain with a welcoming gesture meant for me to follow him there to wherever there was going to be.

Made in the USA
Columbia, SC
10 May 2021